W9-AOV-746

MATH IT!
SORT IT!

by Nadia Higgins

pogo

Ideas for Parents and Teachers

Pogo Books let children practice reading informational text while introducing them to nonfiction features such as headings, labels, sidebars, maps, and diagrams, as well as a table of contents, glossary, and index.

Carefully leveled text with a strong photo match offers early fluent readers the support they need to succeed.

Before Reading

- "Walk" through the book and point out the various nonfiction features. Ask the student what purpose each feature serves.
- Look at the glossary together. Read and discuss the words.

Read the Book

- Have the child read the book independently.
- Invite him or her to list questions that arise from reading.

After Reading

- Discuss the child's questions. Talk about how he or she might find answers to those questions.
- Prompt the child to think more. Ask: Look around you. What do you see that you could sort? How many different ways do you think you could sort them?

Pogo Books are published by Jump!
5357 Penn Avenue South
Minneapolis, MN 55419
www.jumplibrary.com

Library of Congress Cataloging-in-Publication Data

Names: Higgins, Nadia, author.
Title: Sort it! / by Nadia Higgins.
Description: Minneapolis, MN: Jump!, Inc., [2017]
Series: Math it!
Audience: Ages 7-10. Includes bibliographical references and index.
Identifiers: LCCN 2016010030 (print)
LCCN 2016012251 (ebook)
ISBN 9781620314104 (hard cover: alk. paper)
ISBN 9781624964572 (e-book)
Subjects: LCSH: Set theory—Juvenile literature. Mathematics—Juvenile literature.
Classification: LCC QA248 .H495 2017 (print)
LCC QA248 (ebook) | DDC 511.3/22—dc23
LC record available at http://lccn.loc.gov/2016010030

Series Editor: Jenny Fretland VanVoorst
Series Designer: Anna Peterson
Photo Researcher: Anna Peterson

Photo Credits: Photo Credits: All photos by Shutterstock except: Dreamstime, 4, 6-7; Getty, 8-9, 16, 17; Thinkstock, 5, 6-7, 11.

Printed in the United States of America at Corporate Graphics in North Mankato, Minnesota.

TABLE OF CONTENTS

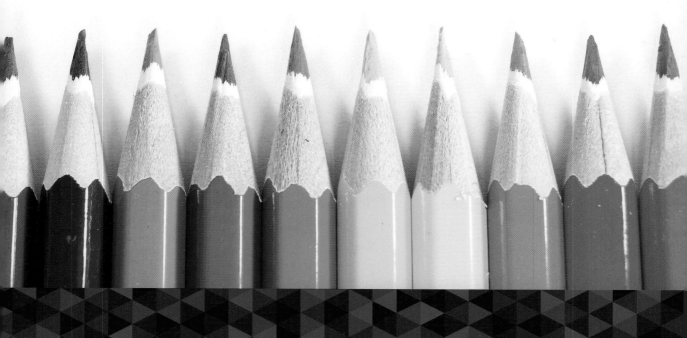

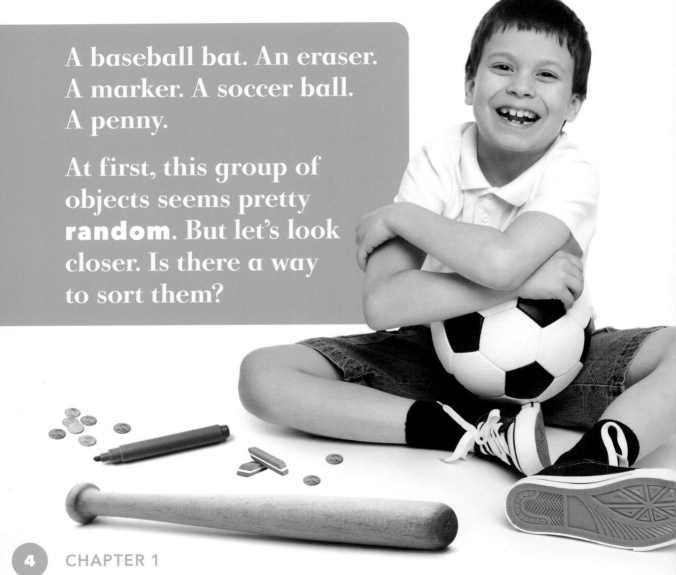

CHAPTER 1

SORT, SORT AGAIN

A baseball bat. An eraser. A marker. A soccer ball. A penny.

At first, this group of objects seems pretty **random**. But let's look closer. Is there a way to sort them?

Yes! Make two groups, or **sets**.

Some are mostly long, and some are mostly round.

Long Items:

Date: _____

No: _____

Round Items:

Some are usually found inside, and some are more common outside.

These objects are not really random at all! Every time we sort, we see what we group in a new way.

Sorting makes it easy to compare things. It organizes our world into useful **categories**.

THINK ABOUT IT!

Do you have an underwear drawer or a change purse? What about a pencil case or a homework folder? Sorting helps you keep track of your stuff.

Date: _____ No: _____

Inside Objects:

Outside Objects:

How many ways can you sort these numbers? Look at all the different **attributes**.

Color.

Pattern.

Number type (odd or even).

Number value.

CHAPTER 2

SAME AND DIFFERENT

A **Venn diagram** uses circles to sort things. It is made of circles that overlap.

How does it work? Imagine you had a big pile of buttons.

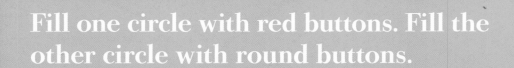

Fill one circle with red buttons. Fill the other circle with round buttons.

What about buttons that are both round and red? They go in the middle, where the circles **intersect**.

Some buttons are not round or red. They stay on the outside.

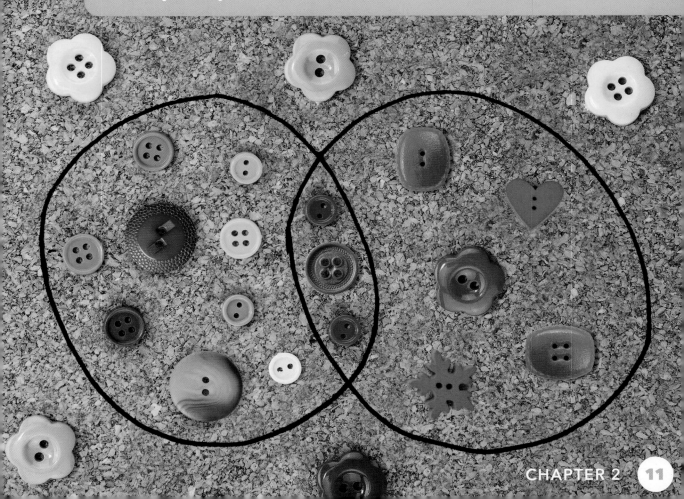

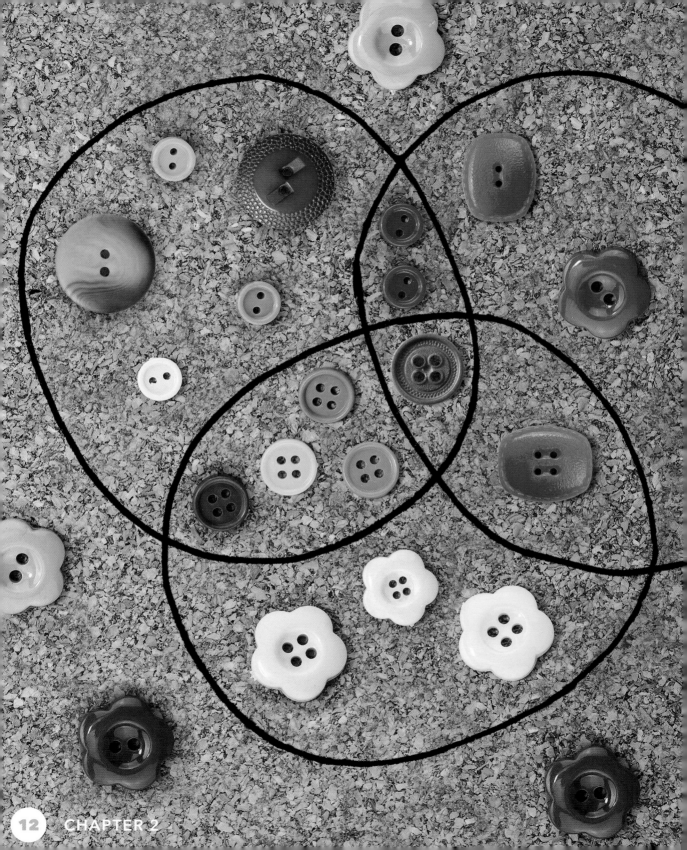

Let's make it tricky. Add a third circle for buttons that have four holes. Now four areas intersect. What does each show?

A Venn diagram can be a handy tool when you need to compare and **contrast** two categories. How are moths and butterflies the same and different? This Venn diagram clears it up.

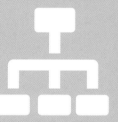

Club-Like
Antennae

Active During
the Day

Colorful

Large

Six Legs
Start as Caterpillars
Scales Cover Wings
and Body
Four Wings

Small

Feathery Antennae

Not Very Colorful

Active at
Night

CHAPTER 3

PUT THEM IN ORDER

Sometimes the best way to sort things is by putting them in order. Who was the winner of the field day race? A jumble of numbers is not very helpful.

JOE: 11.57
JEN: 11.53
CAL: 11.26
AVA: 12.0
MIA: 11.47

Put them in order by finishing time. That's better!

1st CAL: 11.26
2nd MIA: 11.47
3rd JEN: 11.53
JOE: 11.57
AVA: 12.0

Can you **rank** these puppies by age? Which one is oldest? Which is third oldest?

Line them up, oldest to youngest. Now the answer is easy to see.

Peanut
4 Pounds
11 Months

Max
17 Pounds
10 Months

Steve
25 Pounds
5 Months

Romeo
8 Pounds
8 Months

Here comes another puppy.
Where does she fit in?

Now rank them by weight.
Where does Sadie fit in? It's easy
to tell with all your dogs in place.

BY AGE

Sadie is 4 months old.
That makes her the
youngest.

She goes to the right
of Steve.

OLDEST ←

BY WEIGHT

Sadie weighs 12 pounds.
That is less than 17 and
more than 8.

Squeeze her in between
Max and Romeo.

HEAVIEST ←

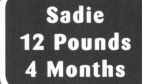

Sadie
12 Pounds
4 Months

YOUNGEST

LIGHTEST

With sorting, solving problems is doggone easy!

ACTIVITIES & TOOLS

WHICH ONE IS DIFFERENT?

Fill a box with five objects from around your home and neighborhood. Find four that are similar in some way and one that is different. Can your friend figure out which one is the oddball? How tricky can you be?

What You Need:
- A friend
- Two small boxes with lids, or sturdy bags
- Two devices to keep track of time

❶ Take a box and give one to your friend. Agree to come back at a meeting spot in a set time, maybe 10 minutes. Split up to collect your objects.

❷ Wander around collecting five interesting objects. Think about how one of them will stand out. Consider shape, texture, and color. Also, think about what the object is made of, how it is used, or where it is found. You may need to collect more than five things at first. You can remove the ones that don't fit later.

❸ Meet up with your friend and reveal your choices. Can he or she figure out which one is different? (Go ahead and give a hint.) Can you find the oddball in his or her box? Try sorting another way to find a different oddball in both your boxes.

GLOSSARY

attributes: What we sort things by, such as shape, size, or color.

categories: Groupings of things based on how they are the same.

contrast: To show how two or more things are different.

intersect: Overlap.

random: Without any order at all.

rank: To put in order from greatest to least or from best to worst.

sets: Groups of things that have been put into categories.

Venn diagram: A way of comparing sets using overlapping circles.

TO LEARN MORE

Learning more is as easy as 1, 2, 3.

1) Go to www.factsurfer.com

2) Enter "sortit" into the search box.

3) Click the "Surf" button to see a list of websites.

With factsurfer, finding more information is just a click away.